Abundantly Blessed

Kathi Owens

BookLeaf Publishing

India | USA | UK

Presentation by *BookLeaf Publishing*

Web: www.bookleafpub.com

E-mail: info@bookleafpub.com

ISBN: 9789363313248

First edition 2024

ACKNOWLEDGEMENT

All scripture quotations are taken from the King James Version (KJV)--Public Domain

PREFACE

The Lord has blessed me with the intelligence and desire to write about my relationship with Jesus as my Savior. He has been with me through many sorrows, much grief, and difficult trials, but also through joyful and memorable times. I pray that each one who reads my poetry will be encouraged and uplifted, and that they will know the Lord as I know Him.

Losses to Alzheimers

My mother has changed from four years ago.
Older, yes older, but where did she go?

She liked to work puzzles, she loved to read
books.
She worried and fussed about how she looked.

Now she can't recall what she did yesterday.
She no longer loves to watch the kids play.

She now can't remember her children, their
names.
She can't dress herself; she cannot play games.

Still her body is young for her eighty-two years,
Her eyes see okay and how well she hears.

This awful disease has taken most of her mind.
She now lives in a home with others her kind.

She still enjoys sunshine, a hug, and a kiss.
But those talks with my Mom I truly do miss.

Mom, Are you here?

With a distant look and a questioning eye
You watch as we talk and we laugh.
And we share our troubles.
Are you here?

When we ask you about our brothers and sisters,
You answer with a quiet voice and wonder
If the reply was right.
Are you here?

When we travel together you look at the sights,
You talk of things long ago--
Of old friends and good times.
Are you here?

Unsure of their names, you listen to
conversations;
You wonder, Who are these people
Who kiss you and hug you?
Are you here?

You open presents wrapped in ribbon and paper,
You read the cards that have wishes
For a wonderful day.
Are you here?

Your face is the same with a few more lines,
You age as your hair becomes lighter,
The eyes grow more dim.
Are you here?

You no longer join in family conversations,
You smile a reluctant smile,
Not offering opinion.
Are you here?

I will always remember the mother of my
childhood--
You play, taking time to have fun,
Making piano tunes and song.
Yes, you are here!

Death in Slow Motion

        she lays in the bed now
straight gray hair against the pure white
pillowcase
        her facial expression a blank stare
        cloudy blue eyes open but not seeing
the ruddy cheekbones accent the sunken eyes
        with no teeth, her chin pronounced
        her hands clutch the poseys
blue veins and bony knuckles protrude
        thin arms marked with age spots
        show from beneath her hospital gown
her legs without muscle or fat
like a tree branch with wrinkled gauze draped
over
        she doesn't move or turn or talk
        no longer in a world of reality

        dying

            ever

            so

            slowly.

Mother and Daughter

The special memories that bind together a
mother and her daughter:
    The mother remembers...
        The first time she sees her tiny face
        Her little hand gripping her finger
        Her soft breathing, as she sleeps in her
arms
        Her smiles and giggles
    Each step she takes toward becoming a
woman.

    The daughter remembers...
        The comfort of her mother's arms and
voice
        Her strength in trying times
        Her wisdom and enjoyment of life
        Her example as a mother and as a
Christian
    Each way she had of making her feel most
special.

    Together they remember...
        Times they cried together
        Fun ways and special days
        Sharing secrets

Times of great blessings.

A mother who has a daughter has a lifelong friend!

Margaret

"Who can find a virtuous woman?
For her price is far above rubies."
   She was faithful in prayer,
   Humble in service,
   Raising her crops,
   Always a willing servant.

"She...worketh willingly with her hands"
Stitching and sewing
   Both clothing and quilts
   "She...giveth meat to her household"
   Serving her sister
   Or a wayfaring stranger.

"She reacheth forth her hands to the needy"
Knowing man's greatest need,
   In her wisdom
   Telling each one of Christ
   With her words
   And with her life.

"Strength and honour are her clothing"
Faithful in service
   Quick to dispel gossip,
   Teaching the younger women,

Loving children
And her cat.

"She openeth her mouth with wisdom;
And in her tongue is the law of kindness."
    She spoke always of Christ.
    With a heavy heart she felt for others--
    Their sorrows,
    Their losses.

"...A woman that feareth the Lord,
She shall be praised."
    She is now with her Lord,
    Sharing a wonderful place in glory
    Saved by His grace
    Singing His praises.

The Shoes, The Shoes

In September, 2017, I visited the Holocaust
Museum in Washington, D.C. What I saw there
will be forever embedded in my mind and heart.
What evil lurks in the heart of man!

The people were merchants, factory workers,
students, toddlers;
The shoes told the story.

The people were writers, scientists, teachers,
bankers;
The shoes told the story.

They walked the streets of Germany, Austria,
Italy, Poland;
The shoes told the story.

They walked to church, to synagogue, to market,
to a friend's house;
The shoes told the story.

Hundeds of shoes spoke of those who died,
Stripped of their clothes, their shoes, their
dignity;
Then gassed, shot, starved.
The shoes told the story.

rumors of war

on wednesday the tv news reported war:
    the blasting and the bombing
    in a far-away land.

we hear of it in fear, we hear of it with pride;
    we watch each moment
    with quickly beating heart.

we boast of our freedom, our country, so
hurculean,
    "one nation under GOD,
    indivisible, with liberty..."

oh, sinful nation, is GOD with you in this, this
war of hate--
    this nation of blood,
    who kills its young?

what have you done, america? what will
tomorrow bring?
    who can justify the killing
    of the unborn children?

will GOD see us through this war? will we
conquer? will we win?

an innocent voice of a little girl asks,
"what if we don't win?"

WHAT IF WE DON'T WIN?

Gossip

She told me all about it--
Did you hear that...
I found out something today
That will really flip your hat!

This is news from the neighborhood
She said, he said,
And then this is what happened.
That's the way the fire is fed.

Tell what you hear,
Then add a little more,
Makes the story so exciting
When you retell it at the store.

Think of all you've learned
About all the people 'round the town,
While on the phone, on the street,
Or whispered when someone's around.

Gossip reveals much
About the people that you know,
But you're really finding out
About the person who told you so.

For a gossip will tell tales,
And perhaps some of it is true;
But the telling and the adding on,
Next time may be hurting you!

Spring is Here

Spring is here, hear the frog?
See the cats, watch the dog.
Behold the robin flit and flutter,
List to the sparrow's spring song utter.

The buds begin to open wider,
The webs are spun by the spider,
Animals awake from hibernation,
All come alive in God's creation.

Autumn Boldness

It was there so small, so slight, so frail,
But yet it displayed all boldness;
The first to don fall's golden fashion,
The first to change from greenness.

It stood amongst the huge tall oaks
On the hill with mighty pines,
The other maples, poplars, and elms
Stood as giants in battle lines.

It was the first maple with yellow and red--
The leaves so bold and bright;
It caught the eye of those passing by;
It stood there day and night.

But a few days later, the others followed suit,
They began to change their apparel.
Now all are dressed in autumn's hues
And very soon they will together bare all!!

Our Miracle

This sweet child, Bethanie, now she is three--
Lively and talkative as she can be.
Smiling and silly and giggling too,
Listening to music and tying her shoe.

Loves to read books and color a lot
Won't even consider using the pot!
Her best friends are her pets, some cats and a
dog.
She likes to go "ribbit" and to jump like a frog.

Born much too early and so very small,
She struggled for life as we watched in awe.
That tiny little babe with tubes everywhere
Is now a strong child with not a care.

She sings and she talks and she's smart as a tack.
She can sound like the animals: moo, baa, and
quack!
When it rains she's not down, she won't mope
and won't muddle,
'Cause her favorite pasttime is to splash in a
puddle.

She's been a true blessing, this gift from above,

She's so full of life and joy and much love;
I thank the Lord God for this child so dear
Who becomes more precious every day, month,
and year!

Roger

A man in silence
  always smiles
    visits and converses
    with hands and arms and fingers.

He welcomes each person
  each man, each child,
    each woman, each baby
    with a love of each and of life.

The thunder of the silence
  never heard by him
    only the music of a smile
    and the whisper of a friend with moving
hands.

A Thanksgiving Poem

For much, Lord, I thank thee--
Many blessings you've shown:
Peace that passeth understanding
In Christ Jesus your Son.

For loving family, caring and kind,
For sweet friends as well,
For the beauty of nature all around,
For the sounds of music and song.

For innocent children and toddling babies,
With wondering eyes and smiles;
For cats that purr contentedly,
And for birds chirping a merry tune.

Every day that I live on this beautiful earth,
I will thank you for so many things.
And when I have gone on to Heaven above,
Forever I'll thank you more.

The Hands of Jesus

He put His hands on the leper (No! That man is
untouchable!)
And made him clean.

He took the blind man by the hand
And touched his eyes and gave him sight.

He took the seven loaves and with His hands
broke them
And fed four thousand.

He put His fingers into the ears of a deaf man
and touched his tongue
And lifted him up, hearing and speaking.

With His hands He divided the five loaves and
two fishes
And fed the five thousand.

A young girl thought to be dead He lifted up by
her hand
And raised her to life.

Peter's mother-in-law lay sick of a fever, He took
her by the hand,

Lifted her up and the fever left.

Those precious hands and the work they did
Pulled this sinner from the filth and mire.
Those hands were nailed to the rugged cross
To free me from an eternity of torment.

Blessed is He Who is Forgiven

Blessed is he whose transgression is forgiven,
whose sin is covered,
Blessed is the one who turns to the Lord in
repentance.
The Lord gives in abundance to those His
children,
Forgives even the most wicked who call on His
name.

There is no limit to His wonderful grace;
He saves and He keeps us under His protective
hand.
His power knows no limits, His strength knows
no bounds.
He is victorious over all, even over the grave.

And one day, every knee shall bow in the
knowledge
That Christ is truly the Son of the Most High
God.
Then the inheritance to His children will be
An eternity in His presence, with Him, the Great
I Am.

Born Again!

Born in the flesh, born of a woman,
Into man's nature
Into sin
Into the world
Into the wickedness of the world.

Then God's word, through the power of the
Spirit
Works in the heart
Works in the will
Works in the being
Working salvation through grace.

Born again, by grace, through faith
Born into love
Born into God's nature
Born into new life
Born a new creature, Child of God.

A new life
A new beginning
A new hope through all eternity.

Great in Counsel and Mighty in Works

Great in counsel, and mighty in works,
What power my God does display--
Created the earth, the moon, and the stars,
Under his feet a green carpet lay.

He created the rivers, the seas, and the valleys;
He controls the seasons each year.
The birds he placed in the trees with a song;
And He gave us our children so dear.

But the mightiest task that my Lord did perform
Was the sending of His Precious Son.
Christ came from the wondrous glory above
To live until His work was all done.

He taught of the truth and the power of God;
He had mercy on the lowly and poor.
Then He hung on a cross, He suffered and died,
That He might open, to His, Heaven's door.

But the greatest work I saw Him perform
Was done for a wicked proud person.
He revealed in His word His wonderful grace,
To me, His child, His chosen!

Great in counsel and mighty in works;
What power my God does display.
Through Christ His Son I found righteousness
pure
And with Him I'll live in glory some day.

Kentucky Summer Nights

The glow of the moonlight demands a hush in
the land.
Only crickets and tree frogs sing their lullaby,
The soft breeze sweeps away the cares of the
day,
Twinkling stars speak out, "No worries."

Not a human sound is heard,
The dogs content to sleep in their houses,
Coyotes and owls nap in the silence;
Even the felines are dozing and quiet.

The only sound is that still small voice,
Telling me of His grace and mercy.
As the light wind wraps His loving arms around
me
He tells me all is well, He is here.

My Deliverer

Through the pain and through the heartbreak
My Deliverer, my Savior!
Through the flood and through the fire
My Deliverer, my Savior!

Through the valley and through all danger
My Deliverer, my Savior!
Through time of death and from the grave
My Deliverer, my Savior!

Precious Hours, Precious Memories

What precious hours and memories
Of times with you, O Lord--
Bringing thanks and burdens
Before you on your throne.

As I kneel before you burdened
With heavy heart and tears,
You wrap your loving arms about me
And lift me from such sorrow.

And when trials are about me
And I lack the strength and wisdom
To solve the many of life's problems
You say, "Let me take them on."

At times the prayers are just in thanks
For so many gifts and blessings.
The joy overflows my heart
For all you've given me.

I thank you Lord for times of prayer
For the privilege to come before you--
These times so precious we spend together;
What a friend I have in Jesus!

The Beauty of Holiness

What beauty to behold
Coming before your throne,
Bowing in prayer
In praise and worship to you!

Peace beyond measure,
Joy unspeakable,
No evil can enter
When we are in close communion.

You hear my plea.
You comfort my heart.
You calm my storms.
Your presence and love are evident.

I worship you LORD,
I praise your name.
What beauty of holiness
I behold at your glorious throne!